STAMP 'N' SING™

SING-ALONG
SILLY SONGS

Illustrated by Martha Aviles, Michelle Berg, Rose Mary Berlin, Phil Bliss, Michael Carroll, Wendy Edelson, Jennifer Fitchwell, Jon Goodell, Nancy Hayashi, Ron Husband, Angela Jarecki, Judith Love, Kathleen McCord, Mary Morgan, Judith Pfeiffer, Susan Spellman, Jerry Tiritilli, Kathy Wilburn, and Judy Ziegler

 publications international, ltd.

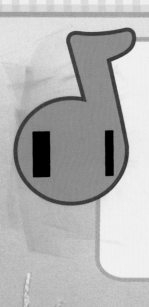

Old MacDonald

Old MacDonald had a farm,
  Ee i ee i oh!
And on his farm he had some chicks,
  Ee i ee i oh!
With a chick-chick here,
  And a chick-chick there,
Here a chick, there a chick,
  Everywhere a chick-chick,
Old MacDonald had a farm,
  Ee i ee i oh!

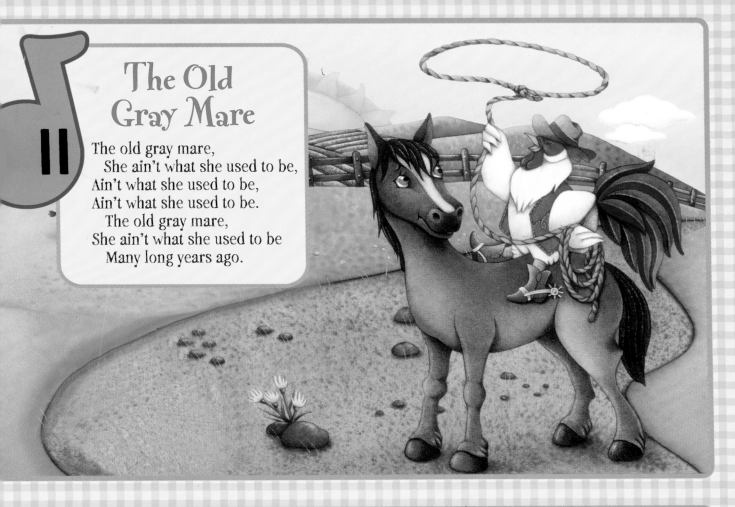

The Old Gray Mare

The old gray mare,
  She ain't what she used to be,
Ain't what she used to be,
Ain't what she used to be.
  The old gray mare,
She ain't what she used to be
  Many long years ago.

Be Kind to Your Web-Footed Friends

Be kind to your web-footed friends,
  For a duck may be somebody's mother.
Be kind to your friends in the swamp,
  Where the weather is always damp.

The Farmer in the Dell

The farmer in the dell,
The farmer in the dell,
Hi-ho, the derry-o,
The farmer in the dell.

Baa, Baa, Black Sheep

Baa, baa, black sheep, have you any wool?
Yes sir, yes sir, three bags full.
One for the master, one for the dame,
And one for the little boy who lives down the lane.

Kookaburra

Kookaburra sits in the old gum tree,
Merry, merry king of the bush is he.
Laugh, Kookaburra! Laugh, Kookaburra!
Gay your life must be.

Bingo

There was a farmer had a dog,
And Bingo was his name-o.
B-I-N-G-O!
B-I-N-G-O!
B-I-N-G-O!
And Bingo was his name-o!

Do Your Ears Hang Low?

Do your ears hang low?
Do they wobble to and fro?
Can you tie them in a knot?
Can you tie them in a bow?
Can you throw them over your shoulder
Like a Continental soldier?
Do your ears hang low?

Head and Shoulders, Knees and Toes

Head and shoulders, knees and toes, knees and toes.
Head and shoulders, knees and toes, knees and toes.
Eyes and ears and mouth and nose.
Head and shoulders, knees and toes, knees and toes!

Looby Loo

Here we go looby loo, here we go looby light,
Here we go looby loo, all on a Saturday night.

Skip to My Lou

Skip, skip, skip to my Lou,
Skip, skip, skip to my Lou,
Skip, skip, skip to my Lou,
Skip to my Lou, my darlin'.

For He's a Jolly Good Fellow

For he's a jolly good fellow,
For he's a jolly good fellow,
For he's a jolly good fellow,
Which nobody can deny.

Boom! Boom! Ain't It Great To Be Crazy?

Boom! Boom! Ain't it great to be crazy?
Boom! Boom! Ain't it great to be nuts, nuts, nuts?
Silly and foolish all day long,
Boom! Boom! Ain't it great to be crazy?

John Jacob Jingleheimer Schmidt

John Jacob Jingleheimer Schmidt,
His name is my name, too.
Whenever we go out,
The people always shout,
"John Jacob Jingleheimer Schmidt!"
Ta-dah-dah-dah-dah-dah-dah-dah!

If You're Happy and You Know It

If you're happy and you know it, clap your hands!
If you're happy and you know it, clap your hands!
If you're happy and you know it, then your face will surely show it.
If you're happy and you know it, clap your hands!

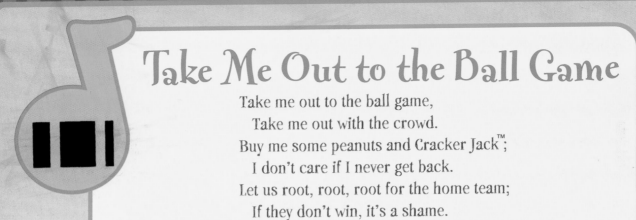

Take Me Out to the Ball Game

Take me out to the ball game,
Take me out with the crowd.
Buy me some peanuts and Cracker Jack™;
I don't care if I never get back.
Let us root, root, root for the home team;
If they don't win, it's a shame.
For it's one, two, three strikes you're out,
At the old ball game.

Yankee Doodle

Yankee Doodle went to town
A-riding on a pony,
Stuck a feather in his hat,
And called it macaroni.

Star-Spangled Banner

Oh, say, can you see,
   By the dawn's early light,
What so proudly we hailed
   At the twilight's last gleaming,
Whose broad stripes and bright stars
   Through the perilous fight
O'er the ramparts we watched
   Were so gallantly streaming?
And the rocket's red glare,
   The bombs bursting in air,
Gave proof through the night
   That our flag was still there.
Oh, say, does that star-spangled
   Banner yet wave
O'er the land of the free
   And the home of the brave?

Down by the Station

Down by the station early in the morning, see the little puffer bellies all in a row.
See the stationmaster pull the little handle. Chug! Chug! Toot! Toot! Off we go!

I've Been Working on the Railroad

I've been working on the railroad,
All the live-long day.
I've been working on the railroad,
Just to pass the time away.

It's Raining, It's Pouring

It's raining, it's pouring.
The old man is snoring.
He went to bed and bumped his head,
And couldn't get up in the morning.

Row, Row, Row Your Boat

Row, row, row your boat, gently down the stream.
Merrily, merrily, merrily, merrily, life is but a dream.

The Wheels on the Bus

The wheels on the bus go round and round,
Round and round, round and round.
The wheels on the bus go round and round,
All through the town.

Are You Sleeping?

Are you sleeping?
Are you sleeping,
  Brother John,
  Brother John?
Morning bells are ringing,
Morning bells are ringing.
  Ding, ding, dong,
  Ding, ding, dong.